The Interview

A PLAY IN TWO ACTS

By Thom Thomas

SAMUEL FRENCH, INC.
25 WEST 45TH STREET   NEW YORK 10036
7623 SUNSET BOULEVARD   HOLLYWOOD 90046
LONDON   *TORONTO*

Copyright ©, 1975, by Tom Thomas
Copyright ©, 1981, by Thom Thomas
(revised and re-written)

ALL RIGHTS RESERVED

CAUTION: Professionals and amateurs are hereby warned that THE INTERVIEW is subject to a royalty. It is fully protected under the copyright laws of the United States of America, the British Commonwealth, including Canada, and all other countries of the Copyright Union. All rights, including professional, amateur, motion pictures, recitation, lecturing, public reading, radio broadcasting, television, and the rights of translation into foreign languages are strictly reserved. In its present form the play is dedicated to the reading public only.

THE INTERVIEW may be given stage presentation by amateurs upon payment of a royalty of Fifty Dollars for the first performance, and Twenty-five Dollars for each additional performance, payable one week before the date when the play is given, to Samuel French, Inc., at 25 West 45th Street, New York, N.Y. 10036, or at 7623 Sunset Boulevard, Hollywood, Calif. 90046, or to Samuel French (Canada), Ltd., 80 Richmond Street East, Toronto, Ontario, Canada M5C 1P1.

Royalty of the required amount must be paid whether the play is presented for charity or gain and whether or not admission is charged.

Stock royalty quoted on application to Samuel French, Inc.

For all other rights than those stipulated above, apply to William Morris Agency, 1350 Avenue of the Americas, New York, N.Y 10019.

Particular emphasis is laid on the question of amateur or professional readings, permission and terms for which must be secured in writing from Samuel French, Inc.

Copying from this book in whole or in part is strictly forbidden by law, and the right of performance is not transferable.

Whenever the play is produced the following notice must appear on all programs, printing and advertising for the play: "Produced by special arrangement with Samuel French, Inc."

Due authorship credit must be given on all programs, printing and advertising for the play.

Anyone presenting the play shall not commit or authorize any act or omission by which the copyright of the play or the right to copyright same may be impaired.

No changes shall be made in the play for the purpose of your production unless authorized in writing.

Printed in U.S.A.

ISBN 0 573 64030 0

World Premiere February 3, 1976 at The Pittsburgh Playhouse produced by Mark Lewis, directed by José Ferrer, starring José Ferrer, Michael Wager, and Dennis Sakamoto. Setting by Oren Parker, lighting by Hank Graff, sound by Jack Givens, costumes by Mary M. Turner. The production was made possible by a grant from the A. W. Mellon Educational and Charitable Trust.

Opened August 28, 1979 at The Academy Festival Theatre in Lake Forest, Illinois. Directed by Vivian Matalon, starring Gordon Chater, Keir Dullea, and Aki Aleong. Setting by Bruce H. Monroe, lighting by Richard Nelson, costumes by Linda Fisher.

THE INTERVIEW, by Thom Thomas; opened April 13, 1980, directed by Allen R. Belknap; set design by Paul Kelly; lighting design by Joanna Schielke; costume design by Giva Taylor; sound design by Rick Ross; production stage manager, Russ Weatherford. Presented by the Direct Theater, at the Nat Horne Theater, 440 West 42d Street, with the following cast:

VERY FAMOUS MAN	Louis Edmonds
THE REPORTER	Lewis Arlt
SAMURAI	Aki Aleong

CHARACTERS

THE REPORTER
A VERY FAMOUS MAN
SAMURAI

The Interview

ACT ONE

TIME: *August 1965*

SETTING: *A large room in a Renaissance style villa in Rome, Italy. Typical signs of decay—cracked plaster, chipped and discolored paint, and occasionally exposed brickwork—lend an aura of history and permanence. The furnishings reflect impeccable taste and restraint.*

The central part of the room is in sharp contrast to the Italian architecture of the building that contains it.

A wooden deck appears to float several inches above a vast, white sea of sand. The sand has been raked into patterns, as in a Japanese garden. The deck holds a low, Oriental table and several floor cushions. Upon another, smaller deck are a Japanese koto and cushions upon which a player may kneel.

In the room are draped objects. Some are apparently covered artworks such as paintings on easels and stone sculptures. Others can't be defined.

AT RISE: *The hot, late afternoon sun is streaming in from the garden. The doors are wide open, but there is no breeze.*

A REPORTER is discovered in the room. He seems nervous and begins to put a cigarette into his mouth, but just then he senses footsteps on the veranda and quickly replaces the cigarette in his pocket.

A VERY FAMOUS MAN enters from the garden. THE MAN is very distinguished and is somewhere in his late sixties. Behind the dark lenses of his sunglasses, however, the strain of efforts to remain youthful can be seen. He is wearing a short, Japanese kimono, Bermuda-length shorts, a wide brimmed straw hat, work gloves, and gatas. A basket holding freshly cut flowers and pruning clippers hangs on his arm.

They look at each other for a moment before THE MAN *speaks.*

MAN. The interview?

REPORTER. Yes.

MAN. Right on time.

REPORTER. I try to be punctual.

MAN. I admire punctuality. Time is very important to me.

REPORTER. I want to express my thanks for allowing me to meet with you this afternoon. It was very good of you.

MAN. You're perspiring.

REPORTER. It's quite a climb to get here. And it's very hot.

MAN. I thought it might have been in anticipation.

REPORTER. That, too, I suppose.

MAN. (*Referring to the flowers he is carrying.*) Lovely, aren't they?

REPORTER. Very.

MAN. I must admit I do have a green thumb. I'll show you my garden later. It will be cooler then. Do you like gardens?

REPORTER. (*Half-heartedly . . .*) Yes.

MAN. You'll love my garden. I spend most of the day there, doing what has to be done in a garden. I almost hate cutting them, but that's what they're there for, isn't it? To enjoy.

REPORTER. Yes.

MAN. (*Begins arranging flowers in the vases.*) So you're hot with anticipation, are you?

REPORTER. I suppose you could put it that way.

MAN. I have also looked forward to this moment.

REPORTER. Have you?

ACT I — THE INTERVIEW

MAN. I was curious as to what you'd be like. I've been imagining all shapes, sizes, and colors.

REPORTER. Am I what you finally thought I'd be?

MAN. No.

REPORTER. Is that good?

MAN. I don't see why it shouldn't be. (*Pause.*) What is that?

REPORTER. A tape recorder.

MAN. Did you intend to use it for the interview?

REPORTER. Yes, I did.

MAN. I have never had my voice recorded, and I do not intend to do it now.

REPORTER. It prevents any misquotes. I find it indispensible.

MAN. I thought I made it quite clear in my correspondence that a recorder was prohibited.

REPORTER. If you had, I would have . . .

MAN. Since it is a stipulation I make to all inquiries concerning interviews, I am positive I did not neglect to include it along with my invitation to you.

REPORTER. In my case you did neglect to mention that fact, but I will, naturally, concede to your wishes.

MAN. (*He glares at* THE REPORTER *for a moment.*) Do you have a pencil and a piece of paper?

REPORTER. No. (*He grins.*) But I do have a ball point and a small notebook.

MAN. (*He glares again.*) Then if you wish to remain here this afternoon, I suggest you use them.

REPORTER. Of course. Anything you wish.

MAN. You've arranged accommodations?

REPORTER. Yes.

MAN. Comfortable, I hope?

REPORTER. They're fine.

MAN. A hotel?

REPORTER. Yes. I got it through a travel agent back home.

MAN. *Pensione* are best, of course . . . more informal and closer to the way the people really live. It's not too plastic, is it?

REPORTER. No. It's fine.

MAN. What do you think of my motif?

REPORTER. Quite unusual for an Italian villa, isn't it?

MAN. Yes. Did you have any trouble finding it?

REPORTER. Not really. The directions in your letter were quite explicit. It's really a magnificent place.

MAN. (*Crossing to* REPORTER.) It's late sixteenth century by an architect who was strongly influenced by Giacomo Della Porta, a Frank Lloyd Wright of his time. I like it because of the view. On a very clear morning you can see the Mediterranean. Do you know that your fly is open?

REPORTER. (*Quickly zipping it up.*) Oh, my God!

MAN. Didn't you want it open?

REPORTER. Of course not. This is very embarrassing.

MAN. I thought perhaps you did. That's why I didn't say anything at first.

REPORTER. Why would I want my fly open?

MAN. I didn't know. It seemed peculiar. It just came down by itself, then?

REPORTER. I guess so.

MAN. Out of habit?

REPORTER. I've probably been walking around all afternoon with it open.

MAN. (*Flower arrangements completed, he crosses to* REPORTER.) Don't worry about it. In Rome no one would notice. You seem extremely nervous. Would you care for a drink? (*Moves to one of the console tables where he leaves the basket, hat, gloves, and sunglasses.*)

REPORTER. No, thank you.

MAN. Say, "No, grazie." You must remember you're in Rome now. The Eternal City. You must do as the Romans do, whatever that means. I came here because it *was* eternal, and I wished to be eternal, too. Actually, it's a dead city that has never really died; a kind of vampire that thrives on the consumption of human dignity. It has been very hot today, hasn't it?

Reporter. Terrible.

Man. The Italians call this time of the year *Ferragosto,* the "Iron August," when the heat hits you like a heavy hammer. No drink?

Reporter. No.

Man. Do you know any Italian?

Reporter. No.

Man. Pity. An Italian could help you to learn the language.

Reporter. Oh, I misunderstood you. I thought you meant the language.

Man. No, I meant do you know any Italian.

Reporter. The answer is still "no".

Man. Pity. An Italian could help you to learn the language. (*Silence.*) One of my Italian acquaintances was a boy called Rossano. He was a charming boy, but spoke only a few English words. His vocabulary didn't go beyond the bare necessities of, "I want you, I need you, I love you." However, these few words contributed sufficiently to Rossano's happiness. He arrived here one sunny but windy afternoon. He had been flying his kite, and it plunged down into my garden. Rossano leapt over the wall to retrieve it. He stayed six months. He was like a lovely flower. He is still lovely but his petals are slightly discolored at the edges, and his fragrance that once was naturally exciting now exudes a putrescent halitosis. I still see him occasionally, lounging on the Spanish Steps. When I go there, however, he never acknowledges my presence. I overheard him one evening talking to a middle-aged, prune-faced English woman. He was trying out his limited English on her: "I want you, I need you, I love you." Apparently, she was seduced by his eloquence, because Rossano hailed a taxi, and off they went into that busy traffic that swirls like a mechanical whirlwind around Piazza di Spagna. I wondered as I stood there, where he might take her. Probably, it had been decided to go to her place . . . somewhere on the Via Veneto. But before that—since she *was* English—they would stop at one of the sidewalk cafes and get to know one another. He would be busy lighting the cigarettes she nervously popped into her mouth from a gleaming, plain, gold case. He would remain busy all night, too, and more than likely would extend the one night stay into several. Then he would return to Piazza di Spagna to lounge on the steps again, the Spanish Steps, and quietly and nonchalantly remove filter-tipped cigarettes from a gleaming, plain, gold case he had not had before (*Pause*.) Say, *"No, grazie."* You must remember you're in Roma.

REPORTER. I'll try to remember.

MAN. Have you been here before?

REPORTER. No, this is my first time in Rome. I arrived by plane this morning.

MAN. There is so much here in Roma for you to see, to experience, to understand.

REPORTER. I plan to take advantage of this opportunity, but my main concern, of course, is the interview.

MAN. You must take a bus to the Old Appian Way, *Via Appia Antica*. It stretches out for miles beyond the ancient walls of the city. Get off the bus, which will only take you along the paved road, and then walk by yourself to where the flagstones begin. Crumbling monuments and statues line the way, and slender poplars give you shade and protection from the hot sun. It is as though you took a step into the past. And just when you think that here the Eternal fire has not been extinguished, you suddenly discover that everywhere . . . are thousands of used prophylactics; their tubular skins no longer inflated by passion, the deterred sperm now sterile, flung among antiquity by the thoughtless, ignorant descendents of Huns, who, like their forefathers, continue to wreck the temples, desecrate the holy,

ACT I — THE INTERVIEW — 11

and screw the women. The old Roman, the real Roman, doesn't exist any more. Where he disappeared to, we'll never know. (*Pause.*) You can go there by bus number 18 from the Colosseum. Also visit the St. Callixtus Catacombs. There are five subterranean stories. Would you care to take any notes?

REPORTER. I already have a copy of Fielding's Guide to Italy.

MAN. (*Smiles.*) Then you should get along nicely.

REPORTER. I'm sure I will.

MAN. Good for you. You are a young man who knows where he's going.

REPORTER. May I take that as a compliment?

MAN. I don't see why you shouldn't.

REPORTER. I understand that other reporters have come here hoping for an interview.

MAN. Yes.

REPORTER. But that you had them dismissed shortly after their arrival.

MAN. Yes, that's correct.

REPORTER. You found them all unsuitable?

MAN. Up to now I haven't found the right person.

REPORTER. What kind of person are you looking for?

MAN. Optimistically, someone much like yourself.

REPORTER. I have been puzzled about why I've been chosen.

MAN. Puzzled?

REPORTER. I'm honored, of course, but I am an unknown.

MAN. There's really no mystery as to why I chose you. I saw your name. I said it to myself several times. I even screamed it once or twice. It reverberated nicely against the walls. The wind chime in the doorway tinkled its approval. You were chosen.

REPORTER. You chose me because you liked the sound of my name?

MAN. My eardrums enjoy having affairs with consonants and vowels.

REPORTER. Rather unorthodox way of choosing someone, isn't it?

MAN. Unorthodox, is it?

REPORTER. It would have been more gratifying, of course, to think it was because of my writing. . . . but I'm glad you chose me.

MAN. Unorthodox or not, is that right?

REPORTER. Yes. There are well-known reporters who would give anything for this interview.

MAN. I can well imagine. That's a sign.

REPORTER. What is?

MAN. It takes a little special effort to have fingernails so clean. It takes someone with a strong incentive to make the proper impression.

REPORTER. And how are your fingernails?

MAN. Immaculate . . . like yours. At college you must have written for the school newspaper—the editor, perhaps—writing rebellious articles about the excessive authority of the school bureaucracy.

REPORTER. Very close.

MAN. And a job at night to help meet expenses.

REPORTER. Two jobs.

MAN. Admirable. And I bet even then you kept your fingernails nice and clean.

REPORTER. That's right.

MAN. And now you're here.

REPORTER. Yes, thanks to you. I've always admired you.

MAN. Really?

REPORTER. Yes. I consider you one of the few men in the world today who can truly be called a Renaissance Man. I've read all your novels and possess a pretty good collection of your music. This is very exciting for me.

MAN. You're awed.

REPORTER. Odd?

ACT I   **THE INTERVIEW**   13

MAN. Awed.

REPORTER. Oh, yes, I am. Really awed.

MAN. You mustn't be. My good fortune has always seemed to me to be merely a whim of fate. I could just as easily have been . . . well, almost anyone. You say you arrived this morning by plane? You must be exhausted. They say the time change warps the mind and drains the energy. I never fly. When I do travel, which is seldom nowadays, I take a ship. Much more civilized.

REPORTER. I got a few hours sleep on the plane.

MAN. Then we shan't make our first meeting too long. I must warn you of one thing.

REPORTER. What's that?

MAN. I want to make sure I've made the right choice.

REPORTER. You're not quite sure of me yet?

MAN. I may not wish to continue the interview beyond this afternoon.

REPORTER. Oh, I see. If that's the way you want it, that's the way it'll be.

MAN. That's the way I want it.

REPORTER. Then, that's the way it'll be.

MAN. Are you a bachelor, or are you married?

REPORTER. I'm a bachelor.

MAN. No entanglements?

REPORTER. No.

MAN. Good for you. You're emotionally stable.

REPORTER. That's right.

MAN. Good for you. Marriage out of the question? Confirmed bachelorhood?

REPORTER. For the time being.

MAN. I see. Your avoidance of marriage is self-imposed in order that you might sow a few wild oats. Right?

REPORTER. It's just that I haven't much money in the bank.

MAN. You're very practical. Nice to have things so well planned. Must give you a secure feeling.

REPORTER. I have a superstition about security.

MAN. What is that?

REPORTER. Never feel too secure because the minute you do, something happens to wreck everything. It was like a little while ago. Just when I thought I had relaxed and felt confident about our meeting, I found my zipper down. It always happens like that. I'm always on guard . . .

MAN. For the unexpected.

REPORTER. Yes. Right. The fly is always the first thing a man checks. But I was too occupied with worrying about you and what I'd say . . . what you'd say . . . and I forgot about the detail. And the detail screwed me.

MAN. Did it?

REPORTER. But I'm okay now.

MAN. Back on the emotionally stable and practical track.

REPORTER. I'm fine.

MAN. Good for you. (*Pause*.) I think I need a drink. Would you care for one? I only serve sake. I serve it ice cold to the horror of my companion, Samurai. (*He walks to the gong and strikes it*.) I love Japan and the Japanese people. I would live there, but I'm deathly afraid of earthquakes. It's a lingering childhood fear caused by a nurse who rocked my crib spasmodically. Later I learned she was an alcoholic, which explains why I hate the smell of whiskey. Sake is a beer, you know. It is a beer made from rice.

REPORTER. Perhaps I will have a little.

MAN. You'll love it. Where the hell is he? He's usually so prompt. (*Strikes the gong again*.) He knows how I hate beating this monstrosity, but it makes him happy. (SAMURAI *enters. He is dressed in a traditional Japanese man's costume and wears a sword at his side*.) Sake for two. (SAMURAI *bows and exits*.) Samurai was a kamikaze during the War. The reason he is still alive is because he refused to crash his plane into the side of an American destroyer. Instead, he flew to Guam and gave himself up. He has lost all respect for himself. I call him Samurai because of the sword he always carries to protect me from the evil Romans. He respects them even less than he does himself. He terrorized Rossano. He chased him about the house with the sword held high over the poor boy's head. Rossano would race from room to room screaming, "I want you, I need you, I love you!" Rossano used those words for all occasions. (SAMURAI *enters with a tray upon which is the ice cold sake and two cups. He crosses the footbridge to the Oriental table, where he ceremoniously places the two cups on the table, pours some of the sake, bows, and then exits, taking the tray with him but leaving the sake pitcher on the table.*) It's difficult to think of him as a begoggled warrior; his silk scarf wound about his neck, whipping in the wind as his plane soared into an Okinawan sky. What must . . . have . . . gone . . . through . . . his . . . mind? (*Pause.*)

REPORTER. May I ask you something?

MAN. That's what you're here for, isn't it?

REPORTER. I'm curious about what you have concealed under the drapes.

MAN. Oh, yes. I can see where that might arouse your curiosity. I should have mentioned them before. They are works in progress.

REPORTER. Works?

MAN. This one is a painting—a portrait of Samurai. I have been trying to capture the look in those Hiroshima-haunted eyes of his. He's a wonderful model . . . sits motionless for hours on end. Then there are the scupltures. That one is a bust of Rossano. There are various other projects, all in progress, none yet completed.

REPORTER. How long have you been working on your "projects?"

MAN. I don't know. I never think in terms of time when I'm working. I demand impossible perfection from myself . . . and I continue trying to achieve my goal until it is finished.

REPORTER. You're a very interesting man. (THE RE-
PORTER *begins to take a note.*)

MAN. Were you an only child?

REPORTER. Yes.

MAN. You're left-handed. I read somewhere that most "only" children are left-handed. Curious, isn't it?

REPORTER. Is that really true?

MAN. Someone must think so or they wouldn't have written it. And were you a happy only child or were you one of those miserable sorts who grew up frustrated with hay fever or acne?

REPORTER. I suppose I was adjusted properly.

MAN. Good for you. Shall we drink? (*They both move simultaneously toward the footbridge. Before they cross,* THE MAN *stops* THE REPORTER.) I must ask you to remove your shoes. We're about to depart for Japan. (THE REPORTER *removes his shoes. With a gesture* THE MAN *indicates that his guest may now cross the bridge. Then* THE MAN *steps out of his gatas and joins* THE REPORTER *on the wooden deck.*) We sit on the floor in this room. It's traditional. Also very practical. You don't have so far to fall after you've drunk too much sake. (*They sit on opposite sides of the table facing one another.* THE MAN *lifts his cup in a toast.*) To the interview!

REPORTER. (*Lifting his cup.*) To the interview.

MAN. And to your fame and fortune because of it. An interview with me will be a feather in your cap, won't it?

REPORTER. Yes. A very, very large feather.

MAN. Then let's drink to your success. And to your . . . hopefully large . . . feather. (*They drink.*) How do you like the sake?

REPORTER. Fine.

MAN. I was hoping you would like it.

REPORTER. I've never had it before, but I think it tastes quite good chilled. (*He sips at drink.*) It's deceptive, isn't it?

ACT I   THE INTERVIEW   17

MAN. Very perceptive.

REPORTER. I drink Scotch usually. With soda.

MAN. Scotch and soda. That's a favorite drink among writers.

REPORTER. Really?

MAN. Papa told me.

REPORTER. Your father was a writer?

MAN. Hemingway.

REPORTER. Of course. That was dumb, wasn't it?

MAN. So you're a bachelor?

REPORTER. Yes.

MAN. And quite a charming young man. And punctual, too.

REPORTER. Thank you.

MAN. Say, "*Grazie.*"

REPORTER. *Grazie* I'm sorry, I forgot.

MAN. Are you hot? It's never too hot for me. I work out in the sun every afternoon. I have an absolute passion for the sun. That's why I stay in Roma during Ferragosto when others travel to the mountains or to the sea. The sun invigorates me—gives me vitality. Many people have commented on my unusually youthful appearance. (*Pause.*) I accredit it to the life-giving powers of the sun. There are some who assume I've already died. "My God, is he still living? Why he's been around practically forever!." That's what they say, I'm sure.

REPORTER. I guess I am hot.

MAN. It might be the sake. It's a special order sent to me from Kyoto. (*He rises, walks to the garden door and looks out.*) This is the hottest time of the day. It's a bitch on the main avenues; everyone is speeding home for a plate of fettucine. Would you care to remove your trousers?

REPORTER. (*He looks up, dazed.*) No, *grazie*, Hey! I remembered.

MAN. Good for you. (*He crosses down to* REPORTER.) Have a little more sake.

REPORTER. I don't think I should.

MAN. Nonsense. (*He refills* REPORTER's *cup.*) Samurai would be offended if we didn't at least finish this

REPORTER. So he was a kamikaze, huh?

MAN. Yes.

REPORTER. Wonder what they hoped to accomplish with the kamikaze attacks?

MAN. I think their reasoning was very simple and direct. They couldn't afford *not* to succeed. You know, you really are making me uncomfortable.

REPORTER. How?

MAN. Seeing you squat there with your trousers on. I'll just have Samurai bring you one of my kimonos.

REPORTER. I'm really very comfortable.

MAN. But it's making me feel strange here with my legs hanging out and yours all covered up.

REPORTER. I'm sorry.

MAN. Nothing to be sorry for. You certainly couldn't have arrived here in a Japanese kimono. It's up to me to provide one for you. Really, you'll find they're terribly practical when it's warm. They let your body breathe. I'd wear them on the street if I could, but naturally I can't. (*He strikes the gong.*) And when we're both completely relaxed and sufficiently soused, we'll being the interview.

REPORTER. I almost forgot what brought me here. (*He grins.*) This stuff is powerful. Hits like an atom bomb.

MAN. I wouldn't let Samurai overhear the comparison if I were you. (SAMURAI *enters carrying a silk kimono. He bows.* THE MAN *takes the kimono.*) How telepathic you're becoming, Samurai.

REPORTER. How did he know you were going to ask for a kimono?

MAN. I don't know. He fascinates me sometimes. The Oriental mind! That will be all, Samurai. (SAMURAI *bows and exits.*) Do you like it?

REPORTER. I guess so, but . . .

ACT I — THE INTERVIEW

MAN. You're not going to be shy now, are you?

REPORTER. No. I guess not.

MAN. Of course not, Just hop out of your trousers and into the kimono. (THE REPORTER *struggles up and stands with his hand fumbling at his belt.*) First this hot old coat (MAN *removes the coat.*) And this tight old tie. Now the shirt.

REPORTER. My shirt too?

MAN. Of course. (*Checking the label.*) Oh, Van Heusen. They're very nice. That's it—off it comes. One more button there, and that's it. Ah, yes. Now for the trousers.

REPORTER. I never thought I'd be removing my clothes before the interview.

MAN. That's the fun of it, isn't it?

REPORTER. Certainly is unorthodox.

MAN. I suppose that is the word for it.

REPORTER. Yes, it sure is.

MAN. Down with the zipper and haul away those hot old pants. What do you usually call them?

REPORTER. Them?

MAN. Trousers or pants?

REPORTER. Pants.

MAN. I call them both.

REPORTER. I guess I call them both, too.

MAN. Do you? Isn't that a coincidence! Here, that's it. Lean on me if you like. (REPORTER *has to hop several times to keep his balance as he steps out of his pants.*) I see you wear jockey shorts.

REPORTER. Yes, I do. Fruit of the Loom.

MAN. You like that brand especially.

REPORTER. Yes.

MAN. Now here's the kimono. Oh, wonderful, Samurai brought you a short one like mine. They're much more comfortable. (*He helps* THE REPORTER.) Now tie it around the middle. There. It looks positively charming.

REPORTER. Is it all right?

MAN. All except for the argyle socks. Kimonos weren't made to be worn with argyle socks.

REPORTER. Would it make you too uncomfortable if I kept them on?

MAN. I suppose not.

REPORTER. I'd rather.

MAN. Of course, then.

REPORTER. (THE MAN *lays the clothing down on the Dante chair next to the garden door.*) Thank you. I mean, Grazie. (*Referring to the kimono.*) Do you have these sent special to you from Japan—like the sake?

MAN. No, they're from Newark, New Jersey. You were meant to wear kimonos. Now, sit down. (THE REPORTER *sits down, cross-legged, with difficulty while struggling to keep the kimono closed in the front.*) You look much more at ease.

REPORTER. Do I? You feel better?

MAN. Better?

REPORTER. Now that I have my pants off?

MAN. Do you feel better?

REPORTER. I must admit it is cooler.

MAN. If you're comfortable, that's what counts. (MAN *sits.*) I see you have a half-moon scar on your left kneecap.

REPORTER. Yes, I do.

MAN. I have a similar shaped scar. It also is in the shape of a half-moon; crescent-shaped.

REPORTER. Is that so?

MAN. Yes, on the kneecap like yours . . . almost in the identical spot. It creates a sort of bond between us, doesn't it?

REPORTER. It would be nice to think so.

MAN. How did you get your crescent-shaped scar?

REPORTER. I . . . I think I got that scar when I was leaning over the back of a porch swing at a friend's house and it flipped over. I cried like hell. I also got a cut on my chin.

MAN. Did your friend push it over?

REPORTER. I don't remember. I think it was just my own dumbness.

MAN. This is another coincidence. I fell out of a swing too.

REPORTER. Really?

MAN. But it wasn't a porch swing. It was . . . one of those make-shift things that hang from the branch of an old tree. And I was trying to stand on it while it was swinging back and forth and this ugly little girl named Barbara Finkel pushed me. She had homicidal tendencies.

REPORTER. Kids do strange things sometimes. They can be very cruel.

MAN. She was the ugliest little girl I have ever seen. I've never forgiven her for pushing me. I will never forgive her. (*Pause.*) It's crescent-shaped. (*Pause.*) Do you want to see it?

REPORTER. Well, if it looks a lot like mine, I'll just look at mine.

MAN. And make believe it's mine?

REPORTER. Well, I could look at yours.

MAN. I wouldn't want to force you.

REPORTER. No, really . . .

MAN. You absolutely do want to see my crescent-shaped scar, the one that Barbara Finkel gave me?

REPORTER. Yes, absolutely.

MAN. (*He lifts his knee for inspection.*) There it is. Almost exactly where yours is. Just a small, crescent-shaped scar. Well, that's enough of that. You've just seen my scar; I've seen yours. We have examined each other's scars, and they have made an impression upon us.

REPORTER. Our scars made an impression? What impression is that?

MAN. It proves that we're both fallible, doesn't it? No one is beyond attaining a few scars along life's travels. But more importantly, here we are—two strangers until a short time ago—sitting in the traditional Eastern fashion, sipping Japanese sake in Roma, Italia, our bare legs exposed. (*He raises his sake cup.*) Chin-chin (*They both drain their cups, set them down on the table and look at each other for a moment. They smile.*) This will break the monotony of the day.

REPORTER. You find life here in Rome monotonous?

MAN. There are days when there is very little for me to do. Samurai—as you have noticed—isn't one given to the chit-chat. And so I spend the mornings reading, the afternoons in the garden, and the evenings are for . . . thinking.

REPORTER. What do you think about?

MAN. Oh, that and this and this and that. My garden is my real pleasure. Did I tell you about my green thumb?

REPORTER. Yes.

MAN. I mean the one I don't have any more. I had three green thumbs once. I had an extra thumb on my left hand. Anne Boleyn had six fingers on one of her hands too. I read somewhere that it's a sign of destiny unfulfilled. And Miss Boleyn also had three breasts. Apparently an abundantly resourceful lady.

REPORTER. What happened to your extra thumb?

MAN. I had it removed. It became an annoying appendage. It was a topic of conversation, of course . . . indispensible at boring parties. I was the man with three green thumbs. I was a horticultural oddity. But, as I said, I had it removed. I buried it in an orange grove in Pasadena. I buried it as one would bury an old aunt whom one has loved but finds has become excruciatingly tiresome.

REPORTER. You buried your thumb in Pasadena.

MAN. In a Hellman's Mayonnaise jar. More sake?

REPORTER. A smidgen, please. It's very good.

MAN. *Grazie*.

REPORTER. Is there any significance in your use of sand in this room?

MAN. When I was a young man I visited Japan. Ever been there?

REPORTER. No. I'd like to go some time.

MAN. I made a pilgrimage to Kyoto. It's like Florence here in Italy—the art treasure house of Japan. I met a man there who had a garden. I was ushered into the garden through a low door; so low I had almost to crawl. What I saw was a stretch of white sand carefully raked into lovely currents and waves. There were rocks scattered about like islands in a great white sea. In that garden . . . I slowly became aware of the profundity of my limitations. I have attempted to re-create the essence of that garden here in this room.

REPORTER. What limitations?

MAN. Mine. As a man. I went back to Japan immediately after the War. The sight of Hiroshima and Nagasaki terrified me so I again traveled to Kyoto. Thank the gods it had been spared.

REPORTER. Was the garden still there? Did you visit it again?

MAN. Oh, yes, it was still there. It was as if time had stood still.

REPORTER. And is that where you met Samurai?

MAN. Yes. In Kyoto.

REPORTER. Are the other rooms of your villa furnished in this Oriental flavor?

MAN. No. I have several rooms in Renaissance, one in Baroque, one in Early American with chintz curtains up at the windows, and one in Late Prehistoric.

REPORTER. Ha! (*He laughs again, but is met with a sobering look from* THE MAN.) You're kidding, aren't you? You don't really have the rooms fixed up that way, do you?

MAN. Perhaps you'll find out later. (*Pause*.) You don't happen to have three of anything, do you?

REPORTER. As a matter of fact, I do.

MAN. Really, what?

REPORTER. (*Short pause.*) Perhaps you'll find out later. (THE MAN *laughs.*) May I smoke?

MAN. No.

REPORTER. Oh.

MAN. Do you enjoy cigarettes very much?

REPORTER. Yes.

MAN. That's too bad. (*Silence.*)

REPORTER. So.

MAN. So. (*Pause.*) What I would like to know . . . Would you want me just to follow a straight line along my own story, or would you rather I elaborate on some of the personalities—the celebrities—I have come in contact with during my career?

REPORTER. I don't see why you shouldn't elaborate on them a little. For example, I'm sure during the years you spent in Hollywood as a film writer . . .

MAN. My writing career in Hollywood was quite brief. It was rather disconcerting to have some pimply-faced neophyte tell you that you didn't understand the character's motivations when it was a screen version of your own novel.

REPORTER. But, if anyone contributed something to your philosophy of life . . . ah . . . you know what I mean . . .

MAN. You think I should discuss it in the interview.

REPORTER. Most certainly.

MAN. Like Marguarita Del Mar, for instance. Would you care to take any notes? Feel free, if you like. (THE REPORTER *runs up to where he has left his jacket and takes out the ball point pen and the notebook.*)

REPORTER. Marguarita, who?

MAN. Del Mar. Actually she was a contessa . . . married to a Spanish nobleman who leapt off the top of the Washington Monument. He was only thirty-two and as handsome as the devil himself.

REPORTER. Del Mar . . . two words or one?

ACT I THE INTERVIEW 25

MAN. Two. Capital "D" "e" "l"—one "l"; capital "M" "a" one "r": Del Mar. She was a fascinating girl. Wanted to make love every minute of the day.

REPORTER. She was obsessed by love?

MAN. She was possessed by love.

REPORTER. She was possessed by love.

MAN. There was only one problem with Marguarita.

REPORTER. She was possessed by love and she had a problem. What was the problem?

MAN. She had to have it in a sink.

REPORTER. In the sink?

MAN. An ordinary, porcelain kitchen sink. She rejected anything other than an ordinary porcelain kitchen sink. It was a fixation with her, and eventually she was driven mad by it. It seems that when she had been about ten years old, she was seduced by a plumber. This terrible incident made such an imprint that she believed the sink was the most natural place for it. Now, of course, her sex-life is completely shot to hell. She's reaching eighty and is too damn feeble to climb up into the sink. I've often though about her Spanish nobleman, the one who leapt off the Washington Monument. Such a gallant-looking fellow and so dignified. It has always been difficult for me to imagine their wedding night—Marguarita in her loveliest negligee, up in a sink, and the Count trying to figure out how he was going to get up there with her. Then, of course, there were all those spigots and . . .

REPORTER. Well, that wasn't the kind of elaboration I was speaking of.

MAN. No, I didn't think you were. That's why I used it as an example of what I won't give you in the interview. I think I should stick straight to my own story. What do you think?

REPORTER. Well, we could reserve that story in case we needed it.

MAN. It's clear to me now, so I shan't hold things up

by going off the beaten track. But you must admit that Marguarita and her sink is a fascinating story.

REPORTER. I'd say so, yes. (*A pause.*)

MAN. Do you have any fixations like poor Marguarita? Do you like it in an unusual place?

REPORTER. Nowhere like the kitchen sink

MAN. Good for you. We've been speeding right along, haven't we? Have some more sake. I enjoy watching people drink sake because I can sit and enjoy it along with them. (THE MAN *pours* THE REPORTER *some more sake.*) An "only" child, a bachelor, punctual, charming.

REPORTER. *Grazie.*

MAN. *Prego.* Wants to succeed.

REPORTER. Everyone does.

MAN. That's true.

REPORTER. I've wanted to be a writer ever since I was a kid.

MAN. Determined.

REPORTER. Absolutely.

MAN. Decisive.

REPORTER. Yes.

MAN. Direct.

REPORTER. Narrowing in, are you?

MAN. Perceptive.

REPORTER. I can understand your wanting to be sure of the person who is given the interview. (THE MAN *smiles.*) It would be a gift to any writer; so little is known about your life. You've remained an enigma in a world where today mystery no longer exists. There are so many rumors about you.

MAN. I'm sure.

REPORTER. There's a woman in Belgium who says she was once your wife. She has no proof—no marriage license, no witnesses—but says it's true. There's a young actor who says he's your son—even uses your surname, but again has yet to establish any truth to what he says. (THE MAN *smiles.*) So your life is filled with questions.

ACT I   THE INTERVIEW   27

MAN. And what is your life filled with?
REPORTER. Nothing half as exciting or mysterious.
MAN. No wives in Belgium?
REPORTER. No. Nowhere.
MAN. Would you like to have a little fun?
REPORTER. What do you mean?
MAN. I'd find it very enjoyable.
REPORTER. Find what enjoyable?
MAN. Discovering little things about you.
REPORTER. Me?
MAN. Yes.
REPORTER. Why?
MAN. Do you mind? You ask questions, I ask questions.
REPORTER. I don't mind . . . but what possible enjoyment would it be to ask me questions?
MAN. I don't know. That's the fun of it.
REPORTER. (*After a moment.*) Okay.
MAN. Do you want to play?
REPORTER. Like kids in a sandbox?
MAN. Yes. With our little buckets.
REPORTER. Why not?
MAN. And to keep things stimulating . . . a touch of the dramatic. A time limit.
REPORTER. A time limit for what?
MAN. For this. Let's say it will be over when the sun sets behind the Palatine Hill. Isn't this exciting? When the last bit of light filters in from the garden. Do you want to play?
REPORTER. I've got nothing to lose.
MAN. Quite right. Shall we begin?
REPORTER. Ready when you are.
MAN. I'm not going to be easy.
REPORTER. I've already figured that out.
MAN. You first.
REPORTER. You mean I should start now?
MAN. Ready when you are.
REPORTER. I'm not going to be easy.
MAN. Good for you. (*Pause.*)

REPORTER. Do you mind being referred to as a bi-sexual?

MAN. Would you mind being referred to as a bi-sexual?

REPORTER. No one would care. No one cares what I am because I'm not famous.

MAN. Oh, I see. My supposed sexual preference is interesting because I'm famous.

REPORTER. Yes.

MAN. More interesting than yours.

REPORTER. Yes.

MAN. My answer then is: No, I don't mind being referred to as a bi-sexual. My turn. Why do you wear Van Heusen shirts?

REPORTER. Why do I what?

MAN. Van Heusen. Are all your shirts Van Heusen?

REPORTER. That's your question?

MAN. Yes.

REPORTER. I never thought about it.

MAN. And "Fruit of the Loom."

REPORTER. I don't know.

MAN. Interesting. Your turn.

REPORTER. Have you ever thought you should have been awarded the Nobel Prize?

MAN. I have thought about it every day.

REPORTER. Then you feel you do deserve the Prize?

MAN. No, I just have thought about it every day. Why do you wear argyle socks?

REPORTER. I like them.

MAN. Apparently.

REPORTER. When did you first decide to become a writer?

MAN. Five. No, it was later, I think. Somewhere between five and thirty.

REPORTER. That's what I like about you; you're very specific.

MAN. *Grazie.* There's a Duke of Argyle, you know. I never saw him in argyle socks, however.

REPORTER. You didn't.

ACT I   THE INTERVIEW   29

MAN. I saw him without any socks once. On Capri. As a matter of fact, he liked to go barefoot.

REPORTER. Do you still write every day?

MAN. Every day.

REPORTER. Another novel?

MAN. Grocery lists. Are you dying for a cigarette?

REPORTER. Yes.

MAN. Too bad.

REPORTER. How is your health?

MAN. Fifteen years ago they had already dug my grave because they were told we'd have a freeze the following day and they wanted to dig it while the earth was soft.

REPORTER. I repeat. How is your health?

MAN. My health is fine. However, even we eternals must eventually admit defeat to time. "Time is the incurable disease for which there is no vaccine." You may use that if you want.

REPORTER. You already have. In your last book.

MAN. Did I? Perhaps that's why it was my last book. I'm enjoying this.

REPORTER. Good for you. (THE MAN *smiles*.)

MAN. Have some more sake. What do you enjoy the most?

REPORTER. Do you mean to drink?

MAN. No. After eliminating food, drink, and the obvious other biological urges within all of us . . . what's the first thing that pops into your mind?

REPORTER. Films. I've loved the movies ever since I was a kid.

MAN. The fate of an only child . . . to sit alone in a dark cinema at a Saturday matinee. What star did you like best when you were an only child?

REPORTER. Without hesitation . . . Susan Hayward.

MAN. An effective, but limited actress.

REPORTER. She was my favorite. Who was yours?

MAN. Raoul La Pinta . . . and Marguarita, of course.

REPORTER. She was an actress, then, huh? I never heard of Raoul La Pinta.

MAN. They each had a meteoric career. Raoul now lives in Argentina. I received a card from him only last year. He owns a fast food establishment in Buenos Aires.

REPORTER. Have you ever contemplated writing an autobiography?

MAN. Intimate details read rather sordid, don't you think, when the pronoun "I" precedes an especially delicate episode of one's life?

REPORTER. Sometimes, I suppose.

MAN. Even a fictionalized autobiography such as DAVID COPPERFIELD rubs me the wrong way. "I am born." Indeed!

REPORTER. But it would mean a great deal to those of us who respect your novels and your music. It would give more insight into why you wrote them.

MAN. Of course, I wouldn't feel adverse to supplying information and details to another writer—someone who I felt was especially right for the project. Someone even like yourself, perhaps.

REPORTER. It would be a great honor.

MAN. It would be a prize even greater than the interview, wouldn't it?

REPORTER. I could do it.

MAN. Could you?

REPORTER. I know I could.

MAN. Then we'll add that to the excitement of this meeting. If I decide that I want you to return . . . I'll consider you also for the biography.

REPORTER. You flabbergast me.

MAN. Really?

REPORTER. It would mean everything.

MAN. Well, we'll see. More sake?

REPORTER. Yes, *grazie*.

MAN. (*Pours himself another drink.*) It seems inconceiv-

ACT I THE INTERVIEW 31

able to me that a young man with such obvious charm and attractiveness wouldn't have been snatched up by some enterprising female.

REPORTER. I told you, I'm not quite ready.

MAN. I admire your determination and practicality. Not seen often. Surely, however, you came close at least once to losing your bachelorhood.

REPORTER. Yes. But I wised up very quickly.

MAN. Your life would have been dramatically altered.

REPORTER. That's very true. I might not even have been here if I had gotten married. I would have had to settle down to a full time job. I certainly don't make enough now to support a wife and child.

MAN. But you "wised up" in time.

REPORTER. Yes. Thank God.

MAN. And this girl whom you almost married . . . where is she now?

REPORTER. She lives in Chicago. She's married and has a couple kids.

MAN. Ever hear from her?

REPORTER. No.

MAN. And you've never regretted not having married this girl?

REPORTER. No. Never.

MAN. My instinct . . . perception, if you care to call it that, has proven to be unfailingly correct. I knew it the moment I said your name. You are making me realize more and more that I have not been wrong in asking you to come all this distance.

REPORTER. I'm glad.

MAN. I'm interested . . . how did you do it?

REPORTER. Do what?

MAN. Get off the hook. How did you "wise up" in time?

REPORTER. I just did.

MAN. How? It's the writer in me. Curiosity. Didn't I tell you about Marguarita? Barbara Finkel? Go on, tell me.

REPORTER. Actually, I had to do very little. It worked itself out.

MAN. Did you like her?

REPORTER. Yes. I liked her.

MAN. Loved her?

REPORTER. We thought at the time we were in love.

MAN. But it "wasn't to be." Right?

REPORTER. Yes. It wasn't to be.

MAN. Star-crossed.

REPORTER. Well . . . it didn't work out . . . that's all.

MAN. How did you break it off?

REPORTER. The subject of marriage came up several times, but I don't think either of us seriously thought about it.

MAN. But then you did.

REPORTER. We had to.

MAN. I see. And what was the solution?

REPORTER. She said she'd go back to Chicago . . . her folks lived there . . . and wait to hear what decision I would make.

MAN. Did you make a decision?

REPORTER. It was very difficult.

MAN. And?

REPORTER. And that was it.

MAN. She carried out your solution.

REPORTER. Yes.

MAN. And there she is, married with children of her own . . . living in Chicago. Everything tied up nice and neat.

REPORTER. She had to do it. It was the best thing for us both.

MAN. Yes. Now it's your turn. (THE REPORTER *looks at him puzzled.*) To ask some more questions. Well?

REPORTER. In all my research, I've found absolutely nothing about your family. You appeared suddenly on the literary scene . . . no biography was ever given to your

ACT I   **THE INTERVIEW**   33

publishers. No one knew exactly where you had come from or where you had studied. It's amazing.

MAN. Provocative.

REPORTER. I'd say that . . . yes.

MAN. I've thought that my novels and music should speak for themselves.

REPORTER. But now that you're so famous your background is as important as your work.

MAN. I don't see why it should be . . . but to make this interview worthwhile, that information would be of interest, wouldn't it?

REPORTER. Most definitely.

MAN. My parents are deceased. I grew up in a small mining village in Brittany . . . although both my parents came originally from Cardiff, Wales. My father was a miner.

REPORTER. He was a coal miner?

MAN. It was dark when he went into the mine . . . and dark when he came out.

REPORTER. Perhaps that's why you like the sun so much.

MAN. I never thought about it, but yes, I suppose it's true. Very interesting deduction. I remember that when my father was an old man . . . he lived to be a hundred years old and his lungs were as black as the coal he had dug . . . he would sit in the window and look out at a sunny day as if it were a mirage. (*Pause.*) I don't think I ever used that before. "Look out at a sunny day as if it were a mirage." Are your parents alive?

REPORTER. (*Scribbling a note.*) My father is still living.

MAN. What nationality are you?

REPORTER. Polish. My father is Polish.

MAN. Conrad was a Pole, you know. His real name was Korzeniowski. And what was your mother?

REPORTER. My mother is dead.

MAN. Death isn't a nationality . . . except in rare instances.

REPORTER. German. She was German.

MAN. And your father's line of business?

REPORTER. A provider of sustenance. The friendly neighborhood butcher.

MAN. Sawdust on the floor . . . the smell of fresh blood . . . His cheeks pink . . . the chill that escapes from the meat locker's door. Did he have his own shop?

REPORTER. Yes.

MAN. And a bell above the door that would ring when someone entered or exited?

REPORTER. There was a bell.

MAN. He probably wanted you to become a butcher too. "And Son." He wanted to add that after his own name.

REPORTER. No, thanks.

MAN. I have a confession to make. I am also an "only" child. It's another co-incidence. The scar, the swing . . . each an "only" child. Remarkable, isn't it?

REPORTER. Yes. (*Pause.* THE MAN *pours the last of the sake.*) Well, that's the end of that. I hate to bang that gong again, but he won't come otherwise.

REPORTER. I've had enough.

MAN. Well, I want some more. (*He hits the gong.* SAMURAI *enters with more sake.*) Remarkable, isn't he? Samurai, you're unbelievable. Do you mind if I put on some music?

REPORTER. If you want.

MAN. I think I do. (*He begins to cross to record player.*)

REPORTER. Then put on some music.

MAN. Oh, would you like to hear something?

REPORTER. You said you did.

MAN. I always do. (*He shuffles the albums.*) Let's see. I have Stravinsky . . . Beethoven . . . Pat Suzuki. That must be one of Samurai's. I have a wonderful collection of Spike Jones.

REPORTER. Anything would be fine.

MAN. Would you care to hear Samurai play some traditional Japanese music on his koto?

REPORTER. Would he mind?

ACT I   THE INTERVIEW   35

MAN. Samurai, my guest would like to hear you play. (SAMURAI *has replaced the empty sake bottle with a full one and has begun to leave the room. Upon hearing* THE MAN'S *request, he sets aside the tray and emptied bottle on a side table, bows and crosses to the koto. He kneels beside the instrument and begins to place the plectra on his fingers.*) When he first came to me, I couldn't stop him from talking. He talked for three days, day and night. I'd doze off, and when I'd awaken I could hear his voice before I'd open my eyes. He became hoarse but still managed to whisper. He did not eat, drink or sleep in all that time. He just talked. The words tumbled out like hysterical tears. Then, finally— it was late afternoon of the third day—he suddenly stopped in mid-sentence.

REPORTER. Can he understand everything you say?

MAN. Naturally. He speaks fluent English.

REPORTER. Does he ever speak?

MAN. Oh, yes.

REPORTER. Has he been with you for very long?

MAN. I can hardly remember a time when he wasn't. (SAMURAI *begins to play. They both listen for a moment.*) And do you play a musical instrument?

REPORTER. No.

MAN. The koto is an ancient instrument. The art of playing it has been passed down from father to son through many generations. It is to the Japanese as the lute was through many hundreds of "begats" in the Old Testament. David the King played the lute, you know. (*The MUSIC continues for a moment before* THE MAN *speaks again.*) Are you Jewish? (*There is no immediate reply.*) Are you?

REPORTER. Yes.

MAN. Don't you think the sound of the koto fills the room with magic? You seem inspired, Samurai. (SAMURAI *nods in acknowledgement.*) What is that you're playing, Samurai? It sounds a little bit like Rimsky-Korsakov. (SAMURAI *nods again.*) I thought so.

REPORTER. And you?

MAN. *Scusi?*

REPORTER. Religion.

MAN. I'm nothing.

REPORTER. Nothing? You've never in your life had a religion?

MAN. I once became quite interested in the Eastern religions. I even visited a guru once. It was somewhere in the Central Provinces of India on a tributary of the Godavari River. The guru was an ancient man . . . some said he was two hundred years old, but no one could postively know. When I first saw him, he was seated cross-legged on a raised dais. His head was bowed in some deep contemplation. He never looked up but beckoned for me to cross to him and to lean in close. An hour went by, and then, in a very soft, gentle, sweet voice, he said, "Grab life by the balls." (SAMURAI *stops playing.*)

REPORTER. And then what?

MAN. He fell into a deep trance that went on for several days. Finally, I left and returned to Calcutta where my ship was waiting. When I think back on it, those words of the guru were, perhaps, the wisest words I have ever heard. Have you ever visited with a guru?

REPORTER. No, but an American couple at my hotel had an extra ticket to see the Pope this morning.

MAN. An audience. And did you go?

REPORTER. I thought it might be interesting.

MAN. How was he?

REPORTER. I was pretty far away, but he looked fine.

MAN. And did he say something like: "Grab life by the balls?"

REPORTER. He spoke in Latin and an American priest from Boston translated, but I think it was more like, "Don't grab life by the balls."

MAN. And what philosophy do you attest? "Do Grab" or "Don't Grab?"

REPORTER. Do.

MAN. Good for you.

ACT I   THE INTERVIEW   37

REPORTER. I'm not Orthodox.

MAN. Then that makes you "unorthodox," doesn't it?

REPORTER. Yes, I suppose it does. (*Pause.*) My name doesn't sound Jewish. How did you know?

MAN. I take it that the name I liked so much isn't your real name.

REPORTER. No.

MAN. A touch of deception, then.

REPORTER. I could have lied . . . but I told you the truth.

MAN. Yes.

REPORTER. I changed my name when I got out of college. I felt it would help me get ahead.

MAN. Did it?

REPORTER. I think it did.

MAN. Yes, I suppose that's true. It brought you here to Roma, didn't it?

REPORTER. How *did* you know?

MAN. *Scusi?*

REPORTER. Know I was Jewish.

MAN. I surprised you.

REPORTER. Yes.

MAN. It was the sake. In Japan, priests used it in ceremonials so that they might more clearly perceive that which was unperceivable.

REPORTER. And so it was just a guess?

MAN. I perceived it.

REPORTER. Like a mind reader.

MAN. Something like that. (*Pause.*)

REPORTER. The koto music was very nice. He. . . . (THE REPORTER *turns to* SAMURAI.) You play very well. *Grazie.* (*To* MAN.) How do you say "Thank you" in Japanese?

MAN. *Arigato.*

REPORTER. (*To* SAMURAI.) *Arigato.* I'm getting quite an education in foreign languages this afternoon.

MAN. Was it kosher?

REPORTER. What?

MAN. Your father's butcher shop.

REPORTER. Yes. (*Pause.*)

MAN. Your name isn't Finkel, is it?

REPORTER. No, it isn't Finkel.

MAN. It's a nice name really. I've nothing at all against the name. It's just when I hear it I invariably think of Barbara. She's probably a grandmother somewhere. It makes me absolutely shudder.

REPORTER. My father said, "The name you are throwing away is four centuries old."

MAN. But you're thinking of the future, aren't you?

REPORTER. And the present.

MAN. That's what's important. (*There is a brief silence, then* THE MAN *laughs almost to himself.*) A Polish German American Jew sipping Japanese sake in Roma, Italia with bare legs exposed.

REPORTER. I guess it is funny.

MAN. It's hilarious. Is it fun being Jewish?

REPORTER. Not especially.

MAN. I thought it might be fun. Wasn't Al Jolson Jewish?

REPORTER. And he did everything he could to keep people from remembering it. He spent most of his career down on one knee and in blackface.

MAN. That is jumping out of the frying pan, isn't it?

REPORTER. Jolson wasn't his real name, you know.

MAN. I would think things would have changed by now.

REPORTER. Turn on your TV some time. Watch the news. Swastikas painted on a temple door . . . tombstones overturned.

MAN. I don't own a set. And to watch Italian television would be the final calamity of my life.

REPORTER. I hear about it all the time.

MAN. How does your father feel about it?

REPORTER. About what? Could I have another sake, please?

ACT I THE INTERVIEW 39

MAN. Of course.

REPORTER. *Grazie. Arigato.* (THE REPORTER *pours himself another sake.*) How does he feel about what?

MAN. All of it.

REPORTER. You don't know my father. I really don't know how he feels. He never says much. I wanted to explain it to him once but . . . What?

MAN. I didn't say anything.

REPORTER. I thought you said something. (*He drinks his sake.*)

MAN. Did you work in your father's shop?

REPORTER. No. Did your father want you to be a miner?

MAN. I can never forget the sight of the miners as they came out of the shaft. They looked like players in a minstrel show who had lost the power to sing or clap their hands.

REPORTER. But you got out.

MAN. I threw away my pick ax and my tambourine and left.

REPORTER. I got out as soon as I could. She made it bearable for me, but when she died . . .

MAN. She?

REPORTER. I'm sorry . . . my mother kept me there, but then I left.

MAN. You must have loved her very much.

REPORTER. When I think about her . . . the first thing to come to mind is the warmth of the kitchen. She was always there.

MAN. And the smell of fresh bread. I know what you mean.

REPORTER. She was a wonderful woman.

MAN. My mother was too. Another co-incidence.

REPORTER. We didn't have that much money, but I went to school each day dressed like a . . . Prince.

MAN. You still dress very nicely. I complimented you on your clothes, if you remember.

REPORTER. She really did her best to keep me from being hurt.

MAN. Hurt?

REPORTER. She'd keep me in the house rather than have me outside where . . . I had to walk to school. The school I went to . . . "our" school was on the other side of town. I never had any trouble getting there, but going home was different. I'd do anything to keep from walking home. I'd clean erasers for my teacher . . . anything.

MAN. You were forced by fear to be an industrious boy.

REPORTER. Finally the janitor would start locking up the classrooms and I'd be told to go. As I started down the street I could see them leaning up against the walls and fences. I'd see them the minute I started down the street. They would look at me and then would look away as if that day I didn't matter. But I knew they would never let me pass. They never did.

MAN. They'd present hope . . .

REPORTER. And then they would slowly shut off the . . .

MAN-REPORTER. Hope.

REPORTER. Until I was being smothered by my own fear.

MAN. And you'd think of your mother.

REPORTER. But she wasn't there. I was alone. Those bastards! Those smart assed bastards! Laughing at me! Calling me names. Saying rotten things about her . . . saying dirty ugly things. They'd grab at me, making me drop my books . . . as I tried to keep their hands off . . . and they pin me up against a wall and I scream and kick trying to hurt them . . . hating them . . . despising them. They drag me into an alley and someone holds me while the others unbutton my pants . . . they rip off the buttons and pull down my pants until I'm exposed . . . and they grab at me . . . laugh at me. I finally struggle away and run from the alley . . . my eyes blurred by tears . . . my stomach heaving . . . my books left behind . . . forgotten.

MAN. Crying . . . running.

ACT I　　　　　THE INTERVIEW　　　　　41

REPORTER. Thankful to be able to run . . . tripping on my pants . . . planning their deaths . . . knowing I'd get even and I would run to the one person I could trust . . . who would keep me safe.

MAN. Your mother.

REPORTER. She's dead.

MAN. She was good.

REPORTER. Yes.

MAN. She'd bathe the tears from your eyes.

REPORTER. Yes.

MAN. Warm you between her breasts.

REPORTER. Yes.

MAN. The kitchen would be warm.

REPORTER. Yes.

MAN. And she would . . . protect you.

REPORTER. Protect me . . . protect me. (*There is a long silence before* THE MAN *speaks again.*)

MAN. Well. We have sped right along, haven't we? Shall we continue with . . . the interview? (*Slowly the lights fade to black.*)

END OF ACT ONE

ACT TWO

SETTING: *The same, immediately later.*

AT RISE: *The sun's rays are streaming into the room at a low angle, and the horizon beyond the garden is becoming pink with the approaching twilight.*

(THE REPORTER, THE MAN *and* SAMURAI *are in the same positions they were at the end of ACT ONE.* SAMURAI *rises and begins to cross toward the* REPORTER. *The* REPORTER *stands motionless.* SAMURAI *passes by him and exits.*)

REPORTER. I forgot he was here.

MAN. I sometimes do too. Then suddenly, he makes a move and the illusion is shattered. Are you ready to continue?

REPORTER. If you can give me a minute, I've got to get some air. (THE REPORTER *crosses up to the doorway.*)

MAN. There hasn't been a breeze since the first of July.

REPORTER. What did you call it?

MAN. What?

REPORTER. This time of the year.

MAN. *Ferragosto.* When the heat hits you like a heavy hammer.

REPORTER. Fits. This is different than we have at home. It's more than heat . . . it's more.

MAN. The sake does it. You're not used to it.

REPORTER. I feel like a goddamn fool.

MAN. You mustn't.

REPORTER. It must have been the sake. It's mild, but it's . . .

MAN. Deceptive. (SAMURAI *re-enters with lit candles.*) At this precise moment every evening, Samurai lights the candles. As with everything he does, he performs the duty

ACT II   THE INTERVIEW   43

with a deafening commitment. (SAMURAI *begins to distribute the candles through-out the room.*)

REPORTER. There's not a bead of perspiration on you.

MAN. I told you . . . I like the heat.

REPORTER. For a while the room felt like it was going around.

MAN. That's why we sit on the floor in this room. You don't have so far to fall. Your legs look shaky.

REPORTER. It's been the day. Haven't stopped.

MAN. Perhaps you should sit down again.

REPORTER. Yeah, I think you're right. (*He sits in a Dante chair by the doorway.*)

MAN. Did I mention my green thumb to you?

REPORTER. Yes, you told me.

MAN. And also about the one I don't have anymore?

REPORTER. Yes.

MAN. Good for me. I wanted to make sure I'd called attention to my horticultural talents. That's one of the little things that makes an interview more personal . . . intimate.

REPORTER. Are we still in the sandbox?

MAN. Throwing sand, building sand-castles.

REPORTER. Then I'd like to throw some more sand.

MAN. Good for you.

REPORTER. Why have I been kept on when the others weren't? You dismissed the others shortly after their arrival. (*Pause.*) I'm still here. Why?

MAN. I very nearly did dismiss you.

REPORTER. But you didn't.

MAN. No.

REPORTER. Why?

MAN. Because there was something about you that reminded me of someone else.

REPORTER. Who?

MAN. You wouldn't know him. He doesn't exist anymore.

REPORTER. He's dead? What was his name? I'm curious. (*No answer.*) Was it someone you liked?

MAN. That would be nice, wouldn't it?

REPORTER. That's right. (*Pause.*) Well?

MAN. Shall we continue?

REPORTER. No answer.

MAN. No. Shall we?

REPORTER. If that's what you want.

MAN. I want to. How about you? Not too exhausted?

REPORTER. I'm okay. Got my second wind.

MAN. Then, let's go on.

REPORTER. Your projects . . . the sculptures and the paintings. I'd very much like to see them.

MAN. They interest you, don't they?

REPORTER. Yes.

MAN. I think those pieces are going to be the finest work I've ever done . . . far surpassing my writing or my music.

REPORTER. May I see them?

MAN. Your request is, regrettably, denied.

REPORTER. Can you tell me why?

MAN. It's my sandbox. (*Pause.*) Did anyone ever try to stop you from writing with your left hand?

REPORTER. A lot of people.

MAN. But apparently you resisted their urgings.

REPORTER. I'm stubborn.

MAN. I'm ambi-dextrous. Did you like the Vatican?

REPORTER. What?

MAN. The audience with the Pope. Did you like the Vatican?

REPORTER. It was okay.

MAN. Okay?

REPORTER. Well, what can I say?

MAN. You saw the Vatican, and it was "okay?"

REPORTER. I wasn't thunderstruck or anything. It looks like it does on television.

ACT II   THE INTERVIEW   45

MAN. The Vatican, which houses some of the great art treasures of the world . . . among them frescoes by Michelangelo and Botticelli and paintings by Raphael . . . was okay?

REPORTER. I've offended you.

MAN. I'm not offended. Don't worry about it. What have you got so far? Your notes. Hopefully all those ringed and lined pages are jammed full of gruesome observations and deductions. Let's hear what you have so far.

REPORTER. I've written a brief description of the villa as I saw it when I came up the path.

MAN. You can buy a water color of it in the Borghese Gardens, if you like. I'm told it sells very well, especially to the visiting academician.

REPORTER. "There's a sand garden in one of the rooms. It represents a garden in Kyoto."

MAN. And?

REPORTER. "There he discovered about his limitations."

MAN. The "profundity" of my limitations.

REPORTER. Yes, the "profundity."

MAN. Not just "my limitations." The "profundity" of my . . . there's a difference.

REPORTER. I'll change it to "profundity of his . . ."

MAN. What else?

REPORTER. Then a note about Marguarita Del Mar.

MAN. You have her name spelled correctly, I hope.

REPORTER. Yes.

MAN. How did you spell it?

REPORTER. D . . . E . . . L

MAN. Capital D.

REPORTER. Capital D . . . e . . . l

MAN. One L.

REPORTER. One L. Capital M . . . a . . . r.

MAN. One R. Del Mar.

REPORTER. Yes.

MAN. And her sink?

REPORTER. Yes.

MAN. Fascinating story. And do you have something about her husband the Spanish nobleman?

REPORTER. Yes. He jumped from the top of the Washington Monument.

MAN. It was the Eiffel Tower.

REPORTER. I'm positive you said the Washington Monument. I have a note.

MAN. It was the Eiffel Tower because I was asked to identify his body, and I was living in Montmartre at the time.

REPORTER. Perhaps you said Washington Monument by mistake then.

MAN. Why would I say the Washington Monument when I was in Montmartre?

REPORTER. I misunderstood you then.

MAN. Apparently. We're to reserve Marguarita's story "just in case" is that right?

REPORTER. Yes. "Just in case."

MAN. What else do you have in your notes?

REPORTER. He's been painting . . . There are sculptures and other "works in progress."

MAN. And what else?

REPORTER. "He's evasive about almost every subject I bring up . . . particularly sensitive to his sexuality."

MAN. An observation that I find exceedingly crass.

REPORTER. Am I wrong?

MAN. Go on.

REPORTER. "I feel he deserves the Nobel Prize."

MAN. Do you really have a note with that comment?

REPORTER. No. I just this moment made it up. (THE MAN *smiles*.)

MAN. And?

REPORTER. "Father was a coal miner."

MAN. My father was a magician. He was a professional magician.

ACT II THE INTERVIEW 47

REPORTER. You told me he worked in a coal mine . . . that he was a miner.

MAN. He traveled with a carnival.

REPORTER. You told me he went into the mines when it was dark and came out when it was dark. He would never see the sun.

MAN. Nonsense. He lived in the sun. He was as brown as a Hindu.

REPORTER. You're contradicting everything I have here.

MAN. My father was a sorceror, a necromancer, an enchanter, a wizard. He once performed for royalty. He lives with my mother in a chalet in a small, remote village in the Alps near Aosta.

REPORTER. You said they were dead.

MAN. They've both lived to be a hundred and ten years old. They're both very spry. My father skis to the village for supplies . . . my mother is writing her memoirs. It's going to be called MY SON WAS A VERY FAMOUS MAN.

REPORTER. And the rest of it . . . raised in Brittany . . . parents came from Cardiff, Wales.

MAN. I've never been to Brittany . . . and God forbid my being the son of a Welshman.

REPORTER. Why have you contradicted almost everything you told me?

MAN. The sun's rim is just touching the top of the Palatine Hill.

REPORTER. I recorded your answers or observations as I heard them. If I had used my tape recorder, I would be able to prove this to you.

MAN. But you didn't.

REPORTER. You requested that I not use it.

MAN. I have never had my voice recorded.

REPORTER. Yes, that was the explanation you gave me. Why are you suddenly so annoyed with me? (*No answer.*)

It's difficult to keep up with you. Did you want me to act as if my notes hadn't been contradicted? Would you have preferred that? Is that what you want? Would that amuse you? I aim to please. Okay. I'll make new notes. I can be very accommodating.

MAN. Can you?

REPORTER. Watch me.

MAN. I'm watching. (THE REPORTER *rips the pages out of notebook.*)

REPORTER. It's however you want it to be. Your father was a magician. Your parents are alive and live in . . . Aosta. Aosta. Your mother is writing a book, you say? Fabulous. See? Nothing to it. I can adjust.

MAN. Got me. Is that it?

REPORTER. You can tell me anything you want.

MAN. The sun has disappeared behind the Palatine Hill.

REPORTER. I have as much time as you want to give me. And if you want me to stay on to work on the biography as well, that would be fine too.

MAN. We're going to have a glorious sunset this evening. The heat does it. During *Ferragosto* they are always the most extraordinary.

REPORTER. (*Begins to get up to leave.*) We'll start again tomorrow, if you want. Back in the sand box.

MAN. Next question. Do you have another question?

REPORTER. Yes, I have quite a few more.

MAN. Next question.

REPORTER. I could come again tomorrow at five.

MAN. Next question. (*Pause.*)

REPORTER. What do you find in abnormality that intrigues you?

MAN. Could you be more explicit, please?

REPORTER. Your writing. Each book has as a main character someone who is in some way abnormal. Why?

MAN. Of course, what you call abnormal and what I call abnormal could have two quite different definitions. Actu-

THE INTERVIEW

ally, I don't know what *is* normal anymore. I even heard that Mark Twain was queer.

REPORTER. I think that is absolutely untrue.

MAN. That's what I think. Gods are tumbling, however.

REPORTER. Mark Twain was not a homosexual.

MAN. Yes, I agree. The Lone Ranger . . . Kate Smith . . . anyone but not Mark Twain. (*Pause.*) He did write a lot about little boys, you know.

REPORTER. That doesn't answer my question.

MAN. What do you think is normal?

REPORTER. I don't know. You just know it when you come across it.

MAN. I see. Would you consider yourself normal?

REPORTER. Yes.

MAN. And would you consider myself normal? (*Pause.*) You're hesitating. May I deduce from your apparent reluctance that you do *not* consider me normal?

REPORTER. You are a very . . . unique, interesting man.

MAN. And so in being "unique" and "interesting" I am to be considered abnormal. Is that correct?

REPORTER. You're putting words in my mouth.

MAN. Please don't ever accuse me of such a contemptible action. I would never want to put words in anyone's mouth. I only want a definition of what is normal. You say . . . your postulated opinion of yourself is that you are normal. Is that right? Can you expound upon this opinion for me, please? How have you arrived at the conclusion that you are normal?

REPORTER. By comparison, first of all.

MAN. Comparison to what?

REPORTER. Other people.

MAN. People whom you surmise are not normal.

REPORTER. Yes.

MAN. What kind of people?

REPORTER. Abnormal people. Freaks.

MAN. Oh, is *that* what I am, then: a freak?

REPORTER. No, of course not.

MAN. You just categorized abnormal people as freaks.

REPORTER. That was wrong.

MAN. You repudiate that conclusion?

REPORTER. Yes.

MAN. In favor of what other assumption?

REPORTER. For example . . .

MAN. Oh, an example.

REPORTER. For example, a virtuous girl would be normal, and a nymphomaniac would be abnormal.

MAN. Marguarita Del Mar then—in your opinion—would be considered abnormal?

REPORTER. Yes. Yes, she would.

MAN. Even though she considered herself absolutely normal.

REPORTER. You might think of yourself as normal, but that doesn't make you normal. What you are and what you think you are are two different things.

MAN. And you consider yourself normal?

REPORTER. Yes.

MAN. Good for you. More sake?

REPORTER. You're not playing fair.

MAN. What am I playing?

REPORTER. I don't know.

MAN. You asked a question and I believe I answered it.

REPORTER. Let's do it another way. You talk. You talk about anything you want. I'll listen. I'll take notes. You tell me what you want me to know. How would that be?

MAN. A new approach.

REPORTER. Why not?

MAN. You do perspire profusely, don't you? It's a wonder your pen doesn't slip right out of your little left hand.

REPORTER. I've got a good grip on it. Don't say it! I'll say it for you. "Good for you." (THE MAN *smiles*.) Go ahead. Talk.

ACT II   THE INTERVIEW   51

MAN. I feel very self-conscious for some reason.

REPORTER. You feel self-conscious? I don't believe it.

MAN. You've put me on the spot. Very clever of you.

REPORTER. Talk. (THE MAN *ponders the demand for a moment then:*)

MAN. I once was in a hospital in Switzerland—near Lucerne. The War had been on for several years and still teetered on the brink of going one way or the other. I had been admitted to the hospital with cancer of the lungs. Only a wisp of them remained. The flutter of a butterfly's wing or the sneeze of a centipede could have destroyed me, but just as you now determinedly hang on to your sweaty ball point . . . I resolutely hung on to my sweaty life. I lived. I met a man there who helped the sick. He wasn't on the regular staff—he was someone who voluntarily "lived" among the dying. I remember he had a lovely cascade of snow white hair over his forehead. Years before, he had turned his back on his family and proceeded to make a new life for himself. He destroyed all connection with them. The War came and he had joined the Army. After being wounded by shrapnel he was assigned to a "collective camp" in Bavaria. The people were herded there from everywhere. He was put as a sentinel at the North Gate—the infamous North Gate. Once the prisoners were led through it toward the low, brick building with the tall smoke stack, they were never heard of again. (SAMURAI *begins to play on the koto.*) One Winter morning when the sky was slate grey with an approaching snow storm, he stood guard as a slow procession of hair-shorn, naked women filed past him. Some were silent, some were murmuring prayers, some were sobbing. He told me that you never had to shove the naked women forward. They would move almost anxiously toward the buildings just for the warmth that they would finally give. The snow that had fallen the day before crunched underfoot. Icicles hung like crystal sabres from the eaves of the long barracks. He said he could still remember the pattern of his boot sole in the snow. He remembered shifting his rifle strap over his left shoulder and fumbling with the flap of his heavy overcoat for a cigarette. He remembered the taste of the tobacco and could still feel how the smoke escaped out of his nostrils. He said he watched the smoke drift up between himself and the procession of naked women. Then, his eyes looked into the eyes of a woman. She shuffled past, tripping once in the snow . . . but he didn't move to help her . . . and he watched as the door opened and she moved inside . . . into the warmth that awaited her. (*Pause.*) The smoke billowed out of the chimney—black against a grey sky—and he looked up at it . . . following it as it drifted aimlessly away with a slight breeze from the North. Snow flakes fell into his eyelashes, turning the whole world white, and they stung his cheeks and fell into his ears, whispering to him as they melted there. They touched his lips tenderly as her lips had once touched his. He remembered she would always stop in the doorway after kissing him goodnight and tucking him into his bed, the light behind her, and she would look back just once before closing the door and shutting him away into the darkness. He would feel safe there in his bed, he remembered . . . under the feather quilt she had made for him to keep him warm, and he felt . . . pro . . . tected. (*Pause.*) You're not writing. Your left hand isn't moving.

REPORTER. You seem to have learned a great deal about this man.

MAN. Yes.

REPORTER. He described to you all those details.

MAN. Once he began to talk, I thought he would never stop.

REPORTER. What happened to this man?

MAN. He's still there, I suppose, in Switzerland where the flag is a white cross in a red field. I wonder if he still has the cascade of hair over his forehead? It would be a shame if he had lost it. (*The koto music ends.*)

REPORTER. You made that story up, didn't you?

ACT II   THE INTERVIEW

MAN. Did I? How do you know?

REPORTER. Perception.

MAN. It would be best if you began to dress yourself. By the time you're finished it should be quite dark outside.

REPORTER. You said you'd have a decision . . . (THE MAN *looks at him blankly*.) About my returning.

MAN. I hope you won't have any difficulty finding your way back down the hill. And you must be careful—it can sometimes be treacherous when you're not familiar with the path.

REPORTER. I thought . . . since you work out in the garden most of the afternoon . . . I thought tomorrow I'd take your advice and get the bus . . . number 18 . . . and go out to the old Appian Way. (THE MAN *is silent*.) I saw it in the movie QUO VADIS. Ustinov was Nero. I remember there was this wonderful scene where he played the harp while Rome was burning. Great special effects. (THE MAN *watches him*.) I could do a good job. I really could. I just need a break. Something special that will make everybody sit up and take notice. That's all I need. You must have at one time or another been given a break. Right? And look where you are. The first time I ever read one of your books was when I was about thirteen. I'd hide it under my bed so my mother didn't know what I was reading. I re-read it recently. It was fine. Brilliant. (THE MAN *still watches him*.) Did you write stories when you were a kid? I did, all the time. And you know what? Every one of them had a happy ending.

MAN. You'll enjoy *Via Appia Antica* . . . and don't forget the Spanish Steps. You might find them particularly interesting.

REPORTER. You'll give it to me, won't you? (*THE WIND CHIME RINGS*.)

MAN. A breeze! Perhaps we'll have a bit of rain this evening. A little rain would be marvelous for the garden.

REPORTER. You make me feel so . . .

MAN. What?

REPORTER. From the very first moment we met, you've made every attempt to make things difficult.

MAN. I thought I was being very co-operative.

REPORTER. You make me feel insignificant. Do you know that?

MAN. It's been quite unintentional, I can assure you.

REPORTER. I feel like I'm being used.

MAN. Good Heavens, you did sit through a lot of Susan Hayward films, didn't you?

REPORTER. What is it that you want? Huh? I've tried to be patient.

MAN. Obsequiously attentive.

REPORTER. I told you things.

MAN. That's true.

REPORTER. I can't go back without the interview. Can you see that?

MAN. Perfectly.

REPORTER. What do you want? (THE MAN *doesn't answer.*) I went through hell to get my name submitted to you.

MAN. Did you?

REPORTER. They said I didn't have a chance.

MAN. And I picked your name.

REPORTER. Like some people pick horses in a race.

MAN. Yes. As simply as that.

REPORTER. I thought the hard part was behind me. I should have known. My old superstition.

MAN. I'm flattered this interview could be so important.

REPORTER. There are only a handful of people that would make it so important.

MAN. And I'm one of the handful.

REPORTER. You know you are.

MAN. You must have pulled a few strings. How did you do it?

REPORTER. I did it.

MAN. How?

REPORTER. I waited.

MAN. How else?

REPORTER. I planned.

MAN. You planned as you waited.

REPORTER. Yes.

MAN. And you discovered ways.

REPORTER. I picked up tabs. I put a few dollars in the right places. I kissed ass. I kissed a lot of ass.

MAN. Not a stone unturned.

REPORTER. That's right.

MAN. Good for you. (THE MAN *walks to the doorway leading to the garden.*)

REPORTER. What is it you want me to do? I'll do more than anyone else. A song . . . a soft shoe . . . a few jokes. Hey! You know what Christ's last words were on the cross? "What a helluva way to spend Easter!"

MAN. Are you through?

REPORTER. Please don't sneer at me.

MAN. I'm not sneering.

REPORTER. Don't sneer.

MAN. I'm doing anything but sneering.

REPORTER. I've played ball, haven't I? I've practically gotten down on my knees.

MAN. Please don't get down on your knees. It wouldn't make any difference.

REPORTER. Any difference to what? (*Pause.*)

MAN. I have decided not to give you the interview. There is no need for you to return tomorrow. (*Pause.*) The sun has disappeared, the last bit of light has faded from the sky, darkness has descended upon us. Those were the rules, and you did agree.

REPORTER. You're . . . you're not going to . . . give . . .

MAN. No. I have decided.

REPORTER. I've come all the way from . . .

MAN. And only for one day. What a shame.
REPORTER. You can't do this.
MAN. I'm doing it.
REPORTER. Who . . . who do you think you are?
MAN. I know who I am. Do you know who you are?
REPORTER. I've played ball with you.
MAN. Yes. Yes, you have, and the afternoon would have dragged on for days without you. I believe you'll find your trousers over there where you flung them in your haste to disrobe.
REPORTER. I did not fling them!
MAN. And your shirt is there and the tie and the coat, and your little recorder. Everything you came in with you may now don with your departure. And your notebook. Don't forget your notebook. You have such an array of startling, new information.
REPORTER. The notebook is empty.
MAN. Yes. Neat, isn't it? You are a neat boy. You at least have that. Neat. (THE REPORTER *stares at him. A long moment goes by, then:*)
REPORTER. "Do I know you from somewhere?"
MAN. I don't think I'm getting your drift.
REPORTER. It was the way you looked when you said that.
MAN. Looked?
REPORTER. I went to my father's shop. I went to say goodbye. I wanted him to understand why I had changed my name . . . why I had to go away. I walked in and before I could say anything, he looks over the counter and gets a funny look on his face . . . just like what I saw on your face a minute ago. And he says: "Do I know you from somewhere?"
MAN. Strange way to address your only son.
REPORTER. "Do I know you from somewhere!" I didn't exist to him anymore. I went to explain . . . to tell him I loved him . . . and he said: "Do I know you from some-

ACT II   THE INTERVIEW   57

where?" "It's me! Your son! I gotta new name. I don't belong to you anymore!"

MAN. But you didn't say that, did you?

REPORTER. You're both alike.

MAN. What *did* you say?

REPORTER. From the very first you knew.

MAN. What *did* you say?

REPORTER. I didn't say anything. I just walked out and closed the door after me.

MAN. And now the world is a big, warm kitchen with apple pie baking in the oven. Is that right?

REPORTER. Say it anyway you want to say it.

MAN. And the girl in Chicago. You walked out closing the door on her too, didn't you?

REPORTER. Come on!

MAN. The decision couldn't be anything else, could it?

REPORTER. You're just like him. You never gave me a chance.

MAN. Did you ever want to communicate with her? To atone yourself?

REPORTER. There isn't any use, is there? You never wanted to give it to me!

MAN. Did you ever explain it to her?

REPORTER. You really are a very perverted man.

MAN. Not only "unique" and "interesting" . . . but also perverted. I'm a man of many dimensions, aren't I?

REPORTER. I've got the interview.

MAN. It was best not to see her, is that it?

REPORTER. The head games, your evasiveness, your double talk, your indirectness.

MAN. Don't be redundant.

REPORTER. I have quite a story.

MAN. So you were free of her. (THE REPORTER *mumbles something*.) What? I can't hear you.

REPORTER. (*Under his breath*.) I've got it.

MAN. Speak up!

REPORTER. I've got it!

MAN. Have you? Has she ever tried to communicate with you?

REPORTER. No.

MAN. Never?

REPORTER. No.

MAN. Why not?

REPORTER. Because she isn't in Chicago . . . she isn't anywhere anymore. Not Chicago, not any place. That's why! Does that end it? Does that stop it?

MAN. I see.

REPORTER. I didn't tell her to do it. She did it on her own.

MAN. Yes.

REPORTER. It was done.

MAN. And obviously couldn't be undone. Also very neat.

REPORTER. I have quite a story.

MAN. Do you?

REPORTER. I have quite a story.

MAN. And what are you going to do with it?

REPORTER. Write it . . . sell it!

MAN. You have nothing.

REPORTER. That's what you think. I have it.

MAN. (*Turns to* SAMURAI.) We never spoke to him.

REPORTER. What are you talking about?

MAN. I never even saw him. I changed my mind.

REPORTER. What?

MAN. I worked in my garden . . . then retired for the evening. It was quite hot that afternoon . . . it was *Ferragosto* . . . and it exhausted me.

REPORTER. What do you mean?

MAN. What is his name again? Oh, yes. Sounds so nice. No, I never met him. He's written what? Good Heavens! What an imagination! You mean journalists are actually paid for imaginary interviews nowadays? Times have changed, haven't they? (*He looks back to* THE REPORTER.)

ACT II THE INTERVIEW 59

Some indiscreet tabloid might snatch it up, of course, for a moderate sum, but no one else would touch it. You'd be considered a fraud. No, it won't work. (*THE WIND CHIME RINGS.*) Another breeze! (*Pause.* THE REPORTER *and* THE MAN *look at one another then* THE REPORTER *slowly moves toward* THE MAN. *He stops and says quietly and intensely:*)

REPORTER. I'll do . . . anything.

MAN. (*Clicks his tongue in disapproval.*) That word is fraught with contamination.

REPORTER. Who do you think you are?

MAN. Still asking that same question?

REPORTER. Some kind of God or something?

MAN. Never God. If I were God, I'd be something that I don't believe in.

REPORTER. You sit there like some kind of goddamn Buddah. We don't mean a thing to you, do we?

MAN. We?

REPORTER. You have the world by the balls!

MAN. I had life, not the world.

REPORTER. You must feel pretty special, sitting up here in this house, this goddamn palace! You and your garden . . . and a slave who fulfills your every wish. You must feel pretty big.

MAN. On the contrary; I feel quite insignificant.

REPORTER. And all this sand . . . this "ocean of sand," I think you said. So calm, so peaceful, so perfect. (THE REPORTER *steps down into the sand.*) How do you like this, Mr. Very Famous Man!? (*He begins to kick and stomp his way through the sand in an attempt to mess it up as much as possible.*)

REPORTER. How about messing up this pretty little ocean of sand! How about this . . . and this. (*He kicks at it again.*) Like it now?! Do you? There's been a storm in your quiet little ocean! There's been a tempest in your sake cup! How do you like it now?! What's under those drapes? What's under those covers that you wouldn't show me?

Maybe I'd be interested in finding out. Maybe that would be something worth the interview! (THE REPORTER *runs up to the first covered object and whips off the cloth. It is an easel, and on the easel is a blank canvas. He then runs to each of the other draped objects and unveils them. One is a pile of clay not yet modeled. One is a piece of marble without a mark on it. There is another empty canvas and another untouched block of stone.*) There's nothing! You haven't touched any of them.

MAN. They are projects in the working stage.

REPORTER. You said there was one of Samurai.

MAN. There is, but it's here. (*He touches his head.*) I never lie. The portrait of Samurai is as finished as it ever can be. The marble is a bust of Rossano—his eyes lifted as if he were watching his kite somewhere in the clouds. And they are perfect . . . in every detail.

REPORTER. You have an answer for everything, don't you?

MAN. Always.

REPORTER. You bastard! I took my pants down for this interview!

MAN. Good for you.

REPORTER. Give me this chance.

MAN. You had your chance.

REPORTER. You can't do this to me.

MAN. Can't I?

REPORTER. (*To* SAMURAI.) He can't do this. Don't just sit there! Tell him. Say something. Do something.

MAN. What would he do?

REPORTER. You can't do this. We have power!

MAN. Show me. Show me your power!

REPORTER. I can't show it to you, but we have it. We have it!

MAN. Put it on the table.

REPORTER. What?

ACT II   THE INTERVIEW   61

MAN. Your power! Pull down your jockeys and put it on the table.

REPORTER. Listen to me, you confusing old son of a bitch.

MAN. I'm listening.

REPORTER. Listen to me!

MAN. Go on, I'm listening.

REPORTER. You're not!

MAN. I'm listening.

REPORTER. You must listen to me! I came for an interview.

MAN. Yes, I know you came.

REPORTER. I came, and I'm not going to go without it!

MAN. How will you get it?

REPORTER. I'll get it.

MAN. How?

REPORTER. I'll . . . I'll . . .

MAN. What?

REPORTER. I'll . . .

MAN. Yes? Think.

REPORTER. I'll . . .

MAN. Think.

REPORTER. I'll . . .

MAN. Think.

REPORTER. You're going to give it to me.

MAN. Am I?

REPORTER. Give it to me you . . .

MAN. Yes?

REPORTER. You . . .

MAN. Say it! What am I?

REPORTER. You shit! You bigshot!

MAN. Go on.

REPORTER. You goddamn filthy son of a bitch.

MAN. There must be more!

REPORTER. You stinking rotten fucker.

MAN. Vomit it out!

REPORTER. You butcher!

MAN. Very good.

REPORTER. You . . . you . . . queer . . . you faggot . . .

MAN. Yes!

REPORTER. You . . .

MAN. What?

REPORTER. You . . . Jew! Jew! Jew! (THE REPORTER *slowly sinks down to the floor.*)

MAN. Pick up the innumerable pieces you have strewn about this room and leave. You had the audacity to assume that you were worthy of the interview. And you were willing to do "anything" to get it, weren't you? It's frightening to imagine just how far you might have gone. What would have been the unthinkable—the limitation of your ambition? (*THE WIND CH!ME RINGS.*) Get out. (SAMURAI *begins to softly sing-chant in Japanese.* THE REPORTER *loosens the robe and lets it fall to the floor. Then he picks up his trousers and struggles into them. He gathers up his shoes and tape recorder. He crosses to the garden door and stops for a moment but never looks back at* THE MAN. SAMURAI *stops singing.*)

REPORTER. Is there a way out?

MAN. Dear Lord, I hope so.

REPORTER. Through the garden. Is there a way out through the garden?

MAN. Yes, there is a way out through the garden. In the far wall . . . It's only a small door but large enough if you're desperate. I had hoped that somewhere in that pale body of yours was something worth holding *up* to the sun. But I was wrong. (THE REPORTER *starts to go but hesitates. He still has his back to* THE MAN.)

REPORTER. Will you answer me only one thing before I go?

MAN. What is it?

ACT II THE INTERVIEW 63

REPORTER. Who was it that I reminded you of? What was his name? (*After a brief moment* THE MAN *slowly turns and looks at* THE REPORTER. *They are silent. Then* THE REPORTER *turns and walks out into the night.* SAMURAI *gets up and exits.* THE MAN *crosses to the garden door and looks out to where* THE REPORTER *has disappeared.* SAMURAI *re-enters with a rake. The head of the rake has a straight edge for smoothing out the sand and a scalloped side for creating ripples in the sand. THE WIND CHIME RINGS.*)

MAN. Another breeze! The first breeze since July. Perhaps we'll have some rain tonight. Even the smallest amount would be so good for the garden. (SAMURAI *begins to smooth the sand and then rake it into its wave patterns.*) That's it, Samurai. Not a grain of sand must be out of place. He might surprise himself. Sometimes when you perceive yourself so vividly . . . a change occurs. Don't you agree? So much like the young man who went into that garden in Kyoto. It too had a very small door through which to escape. I had to . . . crawl. Someday he may return for the interview he never got. He'll come at the same time. He knows I'm in the garden till about five. You'll have come into the garden to announce his presence . . . I won't recognize the name. I'll think he's a stranger. I'll come into the doorway carrying the flowers. He'll be standing here perspiring from the long walk up the path. His eyes will be anxious . . . expectant. I'll be careful not to show my surprise at seeing him and will pause for a moment for the proper dramatic effect. Then I'll smile and say very simply . . . (*THE WIND CHIME RINGS.* THE MAN *is standing in the identical position he was when he first appeared.*) The interview? (SAMURAI *continues to rake the sand, and the breeze stirs the wind chime as* . . .)

THE CURTAIN FALLS

PROPERTY LIST

SET PROPS:
Japanese floor cushions
Low Oriental table
Record player
LP records
Cabinet for phonograph records
Dante chair
Wind chime
Japanese koto and finger plectrums
Table or workbench for flower arranging
Vases with withered flowers
Pitcher or watering can
Unfinished piece of marble on pedestal
Unpainted stretched canvas on easel
Canvases and materials for sculptures
Drop cloths for art works
Oriental gong and striker
Sand or fine gravel
MAN:
Costume
   Short kimono
   Short pants
   Hat
   Gatas
Props
   Sunglasses
   Basket
   Fresh flowers
   Pruning clippers
   Work gloves

PROPERTY LIST

REPORTER:
Costume
   2-piece suit
   Necktie
   Belt
   Shirt
   Underbriefs
   Argyle socks
   Shoes
   Short silk kimono*

Props
   Handkerchief
   Cigarettes
   Portable tape recorder
   Pocket-size note pad
   Ball-point pen

SAMURAI:
Costume
   Samurai robes
   Tabis
   Gatas

Props
   Samurai sword and sheath
   Small tray
   2 sake bottles
   2 sake cups
   Short silk kimono, folded*
   Tray of lit candles
   Rake

* Same

6 RMS RIV VU
BOB RANDALL
(Little Theatre) Comedy
4 Men, 4 Women, Interior

A vacant apartment with a river view is open for inspection by prospective tenants, and among them are a man and a woman who have never met before. They are the last to leave and, when they get ready to depart, they find that the door is locked and they are shut in. Since they are attractive young people, they find each other interesting and the fact that both are happily married adds to their delight of mutual, yet obviously separate interests.

> ". . . a Broadway comedy of fun and class, as cheerful as a rising souffle. A sprightly, happy comedy of charm and humor. Two people playing out a very vital game of love, an attractive fantasy with a precious tincture of truth to it."—N.Y. Times.
> ". . . perfectly charming entertainment, sexy, romantic and funny."—Women's Wear Daily.

Royalty, $50—$35

WHO KILLED SANTA CLAUS?
TERENCE FEELY
(All Groups) Thriller
6 Men, 2 Women, Interior

Barbara Love is a popular television 'auntie'. It is Christmas, and a number of men connected with her are coming to a party. Her secretary, Connie, is also there. Before they arrive she is threatened by a disguised voice on her Ansaphone, and is sent a grotesque 'murdered' doll in a coffin, wearing a dress resembling one of her own. She calls the police, and a handsome detective arrives. Shortly afterwards her guests follow. It becomes apparent that one of those guests is planning to kill her. Or is it the strange young man who turns up unexpectedly, claiming to belong to the publicity department, but unknown to any of the others?

> ". . . is a thriller with heaps of suspense, surprises, and nattily cleaver turns and twists . . . Mr. Feeley is technically highly skilled in the artificial range of operations, and his dialogue is brilliantly effective."—The Stage. London.

Royalty, $50—$25

THE SEA HORSE
EDWARD J. MOORE
(Little Theatre) Drama
1 Man, 1 Woman, Interior

It is a play that is, by turns, tender, ribald, funny and suspenseful. Audiences everywhere will take it to their hearts because it is touched with humanity and illuminates with glowing sympathy the complexities of a man-woman relationship. Set in a West Coast waterfront bar, the play is about Harry Bales, a seaman, who, when on shore leave, usually heads for "The Sea Horse," the bar run by Gertrude Blum, the heavy, unsentimental proprietor. Their relationship is purely physical and, as the play begins, they have never confided their private yearnings to each other. But this time Harry has returned with a dream: to buy a charter fishing boat and to have a son by Gertrude. She, in her turn, has made her life one of hard work, by day, and nocturnal love-making; she has encased her heart behind a facade of toughness, utterly devoid of sentimentality, because of a failed marriage. Irwin's play consists in the ritual of "dance" courtship by Harry of Gertrude, as these two outwardly abrasive characters fight, make up, fight again, spin dreams, deflate them, make love and reveal their long locked-up secrets.

"A burst of brilliance!"—*N.Y. Post.* "I was touched close to tears!"—*Village Voice.* "A must! An incredible love story. A beautiful play?"—*Newhouse Newspapers.* "A major new playwright!"—*Variety.*

ROYALTY, $50-$35

THE AU PAIR MAN
HUGH LEONARD
(Little Theatre) Comedy
1 Man, 1 Woman, Interior

The play concerns a rough Irish bill collector named Hartigan, who becomes a love slave and companion to an English lady named Elizabeth, who lives in a cluttered London town house, which looks more like a museum for a British Empire on which the sun has long set. Even the door bell chimes out the national anthem. Hartigan is immediately conscripted into her service in return for which she agrees to teach him how to be a gentleman rather after the fashion of a reverse Pygmalion. The play is a wild one, and is really the never-ending battle between England and Ireland. Produced to critical acclaim at Lincoln Center's Vivian Beaumont Theatre.

ROYALTY, $50-$35

A Breeze from The Gulf

MART CROWLEY

(Little Theatre) Drama

The author of "The Boys in the Band" takes us on a journey back to a small Mississippi town to watch a 15-year-old boy suffer through adolescence to adulthood and success as a writer. His mother is a frilly southern doll who has nothing to fall back on when her beauty fades. She develops headaches and other physical problems, while the asthmatic son turns to dolls and toys at an age when other boys are turning to sports. The traveling father becomes withdrawn, takes to drink; and mother takes to drugs to kill the pain of the remembrances of things past. She eventually ends in an asylum, and the father in his fumbling way tries to tell the son to live the life he must.

> "The boy is plunged into a world of suffering he didn't create. . . . One of the most electrifying plays I've seen in the past few years . . . Scenes boil and hiss . . . The dialogue goes straight to the heart." Reed, Sunday News.

Royalty, $50–$35

ECHOES

N. RICHARD NASH

(All Groups) Drama
2 Men, 1 Woman, Interior

A young man and woman build a low-keyed paradise of happiness within an asylum, only to have it shattered by the intrusion of the outside world. The two characters search, at times agonizingly to determine the difference between illusion and reality. The effort is lightened at times by moments of shared love and "pretend" games, like decorating Christmas trees that are not really there. The theme of love, vulnerable to the surveillances of the asylum, and the ministrations of the psychiatrist, (a non-speaking part) seems as fragile in the constrained setting as it often is in the outside world.

> ". . . even with the tragic, sombre theme there is a note of hope and possible release and the situations presented specifically also have universal applications to give it strong effect . . . intellectual, but charged with emotion."—Reed.

Royalty, $50–$35